# This Notebook

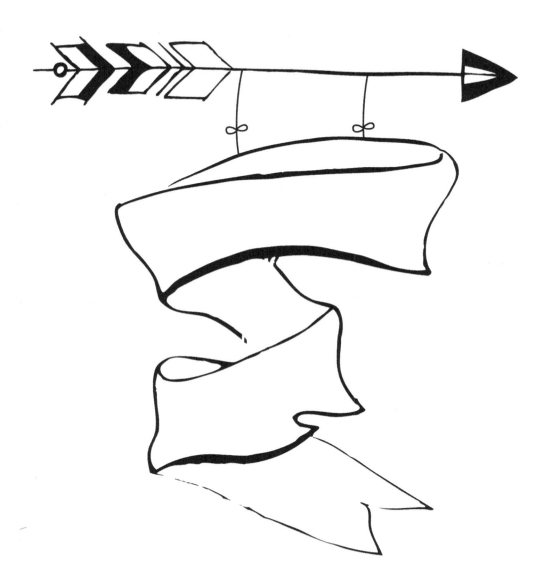

never stop
dreaming

An early-morning walk is a blessing for the whole day

# Time for a Break

## Stress Relief Coloring

Smile
More
worry
less.

be amazing

# Time for a Break

# Stress Relief Coloring

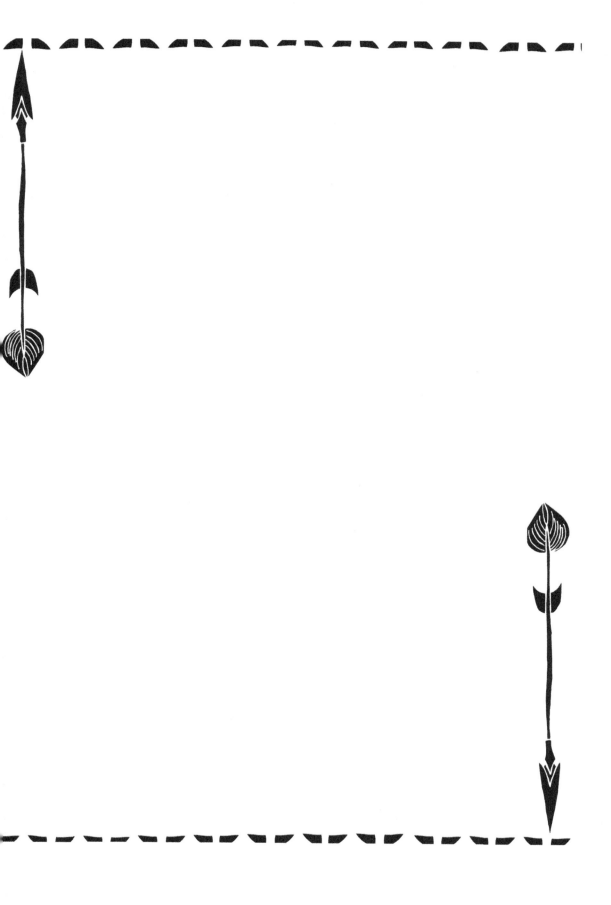

Take a breack
it's
Coffee
time

# Time for a Break

# Stress Relief Coloring

You warm my heart

life is
perfect

2 Teach Is
2 Touch Lives
4 Ever

sweet ♡ dreams

today is your day

# Time for a Break

## Stress Relief Coloring

It takes a
**Big**
♥ ♥
Heart
TO HELP SHAPE
LITTLE MINDS

life is
beautiful

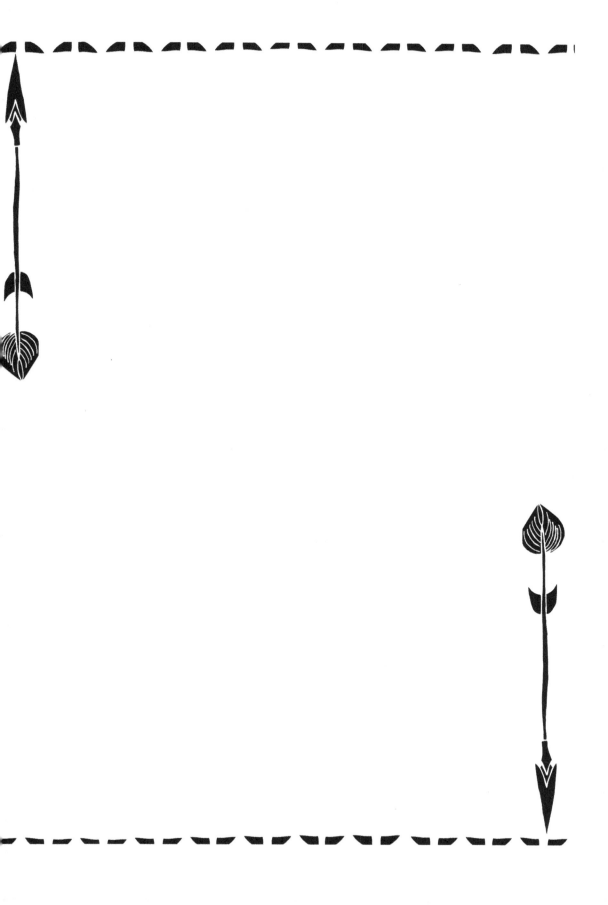

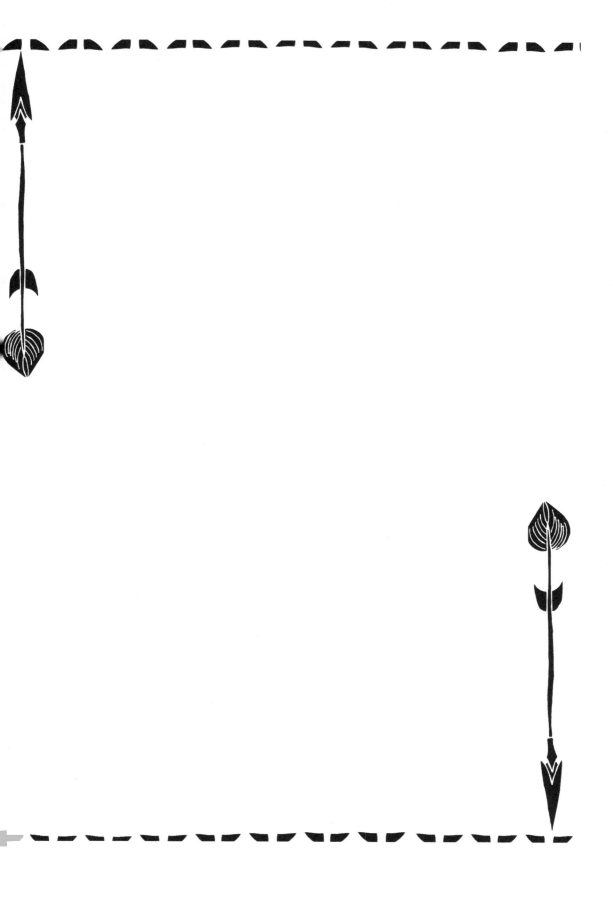

# Time for a Break

## Stress Relief Coloring

don't be afraid to be Great

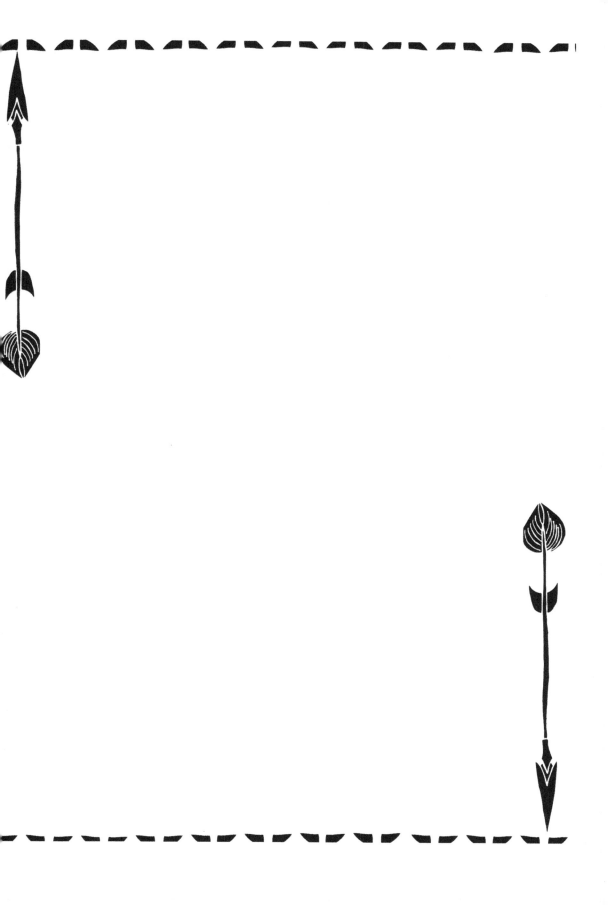

# Time for a Break

# Stress Relief Coloring

Made in the USA
Middletown, DE
07 May 2022

65466930R00057